Lower Blood Pressure: DASH Diet to Reduce Hypertension

By

Evelyn Fisher

Legal & Disclaimer

The information contained in this book is not designed to replace or take the place of any form of medicine or professional medical advice. The information in this book has been provided for educational and entertainment purposes only.

The information contained in this book has been compiled from sources deemed reliable, and it is accurate to the best of the Author's knowledge; however, the Author cannot guarantee its accuracy and validity and cannot be held liable for any errors or omissions. Changes are periodically made to this book. You must consult your doctor or get professional medical advice before using any of the suggested remedies, techniques, or information in this book.

Upon using the information contained in this book, you agree to hold harmless the Author from and against any damages, costs, and expenses, including any legal fees potentially resulting from the application of any of the information provided by this guide. This disclaimer applies to any damages or injury caused by the use and application, whether directly or indirectly, of any advice or information presented, whether for breach of contract, tort, negligence, personal injury, criminal intent, or under any other cause of action.

You agree to accept all risks of using the information presented inside this book. You need to consult a professional medical practitioner in order to ensure you are both able and healthy enough to participate in this program.

Table of Contents

INTRODUCTION

Hypertension or chronically high blood pressure is today one of the most prevalent and potentially fatal health conditions around the world. Among the several significant factors that play critical roles that contribute to an individual suffering from this condition, the most prominent is diet. Hypertension is very often attributed to eating too much of certain foods. Yet another direct cause of high blood pressure is related to obesity which again is the result of a person's diet. Hence it is clear that one very effective way to minimize the risk of hypertension is to have a diet that is healthy.

This over-riding goal of this book is to provide a proven guide on having a diet that will naturally lessen the possibility of hypertension. The DASH diet is scientifically shown to be really effective in lowering blood pressure and it is not difficult to adopt unlike some other programs that claims to do wonders.

The DASH diet has become extremely popular in many parts of the world particularly in regions where people are concern about their overall health in general and particularly so with those needing to carefully manage and keep their tendency towards high blood pressure under control.

It has been medically shown that through changing certain aspects of a person's diet especially with respect to healthy eating, the problem of hypertension can truly be overcome. And the beauty of this approach is that once the initial challenges of adopting a modified diet is taken care of, reducing the blood pressure is achieved very naturally.

This is where this book comes in. It briefly explains the fundamentals of the DASH diet, discusses how certain foods will help in keeping hypertension away, and provides a sample of DASH diet recipes. There is really no need to rush into adopting DASH diet as a way of life. Begin by understanding and appreciating the goals and the benefits. Then try out a few of the recipes and gradually adopt this as part of your new lifestyle choice. You will find that hypertension would begin to be less of a problem.

~ Evelyn Fisher~

CHAPTER 1

The DASH Diet Basics

Defining the DASH Diet

The DASH diet has been specially designed not only for people who already have high blood pressure, but also as a preventative measure for those who are at risk of the condition. This diet, aside from benefiting overall health, is formulated to support the medical treatments such individuals have been prescribed. Hence, the acronym "DASH" which stands for "**D**ietary **A**pproaches to **S**top **H**ypertension".

These are the main features of the DASH Diet:
- Low in saturated fat, cholesterol, and total fat
- Consumption of more fruits and vegetables
- Eating more low fat dairy foods, wholegrain products, fish, poultry and nuts

- Limiting red meat (e.g. pork, beef), sweets, and sweetened or sugary drink
- Rich in minerals such as magnesium, calcium, and potassium

Research shows that people on the DASH Diet were able to lower their blood pressure in less than 2 weeks. A slightly modified version of the diet is the DASH-Sodium which reduces the amount of sodium consumed per day to 1,500 milligrams. Studies have shown that individuals on this diet were also able to easily lower their blood pressure.

Taking your first steps on the DASH Diet

Like most eating plans, the DASH diet requires a certain number of servings from diverse food groups. Different factors like age, metabolism, activity level, and weight can affect the number of calories a person needs in a day, which can in turn alter the required number of servings you need to consume.

Starting any diet can be difficult. That is why it is recommended that you make the changes to your eating habits gradually. For instance, increasing your consumption of fruits and vegetables as you lessen your meat and fatty foods. This might lead into making some of your meals largely vegetarian.

What to Eat

On a 2000 calorie diet, the DASH diet includes:
- **Grains (at least 3 whole grain products daily): 7-8 daily servings**
  Cereal, bread, pasta and rice. Grains are rich in fiber and vitamins which help in providing good metabolism. One serving can be 1 slice of whole wheat bread or 1/2 cup cooked rice or pasta.

- **Fruits: 4-5 daily servings**
  Fruits are easy to prepare and are often rich in many nutrients that are essential for a healthy diet. One serving can be 1/2 cup of fresh, frozen, or canned fruit.

- **Vegetables: 4-5 daily servings**
  Many vegetables are naturally low in fat and calories. Like fruits, they also provide a source of many important nutrients and vitamins. One serving can be 1 cup of raw leafy greens, or 1/2 cup of cooked veggies.

- **Low-fat or Non-fat dairy products: 2-3 daily servings**
  Dairy products are essential for health and maintenance of your body, especially bone health. One serving can be 8 ounces of milk or 1 cup low fat yoghurt.

- **Nuts, Seeds, and Dry Beans: 4-5 servings per week**

Lentils, peas, sunflower seeds, almonds, kidney beans, and other foods of this food group contribute key nutrients that are important to disease prevention. However, servings should be limited as these foods contain a lot of calories. One serving can be 1/2 cup cooked beans or peas, 1/3 cup nuts, or 2 tablespoons seeds.

- **Fats and Oils: 2-3 daily servings**
Fat, taken in healthy amounts, helps the body absorb vitamins and nutrients from other foods. Too much fat, however, can be harmful and can increase the risk of heart disease, diabetes, and obesity. One serving can be 1 teaspoon of olive oil (or any other oil) or 2 tablespoons of salad dressing.

- **Sweets: 5 servings or less per week**
Sweets are a treat that are hard to get rid of entirely, and you don't have to completely avoid them. Just be careful of not going overboard with sweets. One serving can be 2 teaspoons low-sugar jam or jelly, 1 small muffin (plain), or 2 small cookies (no frosting).

The Focus of the DASH Diet

Starting almost any kind of diet is never easy. We groan when we hear of all the restrictions and limitations, thinking about that leftover cake in the fridge or the juicy burgers you'll miss out during family barbecue.

Most do their best to stick to these rules despite the difficulty, aiming to lose weight. That's the objective of the majority of diets, right? Benefiting your overall health is just an added bonus.

This is where the DASH Diet differs from most diets. Improving your health is its main and central goal, especially where your blood pressure is concerned.

People who have high blood pressure are prescribed medications to help manage their conditions. Keeping to the guidelines of the DASH diet, avoiding fat and cholesterol, limiting red meat and sweets, eating more fruits and vegetables, dairy, wholegrain products and nuts, you'll be able to start weaning yourself off of your medications aside from losing weight.

Even more than that, studies have shown that the diet lowers the risk of a number of diseases, including diabetes, heart disease, and some kinds of cancer. In many ways, these are to be expected with eating healthy food in the right proportion. Hence, following the DASH diet guidelines will lead to enhanced health and minimize the probabilities of hypertension.

Getting to know all that, the effort and discipline you put into sticking to a diet seems more than worth it if results in all these benefits.

CHAPTER 2

DASH Diet and High Blood Pressure

Having high blood pressure can have both short term and long term negative effects. Some common symptoms of hypertension include headaches, dizziness, and pain in the back of the neck. If a person consistently has high blood pressure, it can cause weakening and damaging of the blood vessels in the arteries, heart, and brain. These can lead to stroke, aneurysms, heart failure, dementia, and many more serious health issues and problems.

The DASH diet may be recommended by your doctor to help lower the levels of your blood pressure if you are hypertensive.

Blood pressure is a term that refers to the tension exerted on the inner walls of vessels as blood flows through them to reach the various parts of the body. The optimal levels of blood pressure are 120/80 mm Hg. The 120 refers to the systolic blood pressure (the highest amount of tension exerted on the walls of blood vessels as the heart beats). On the other hand, the 80 refers to the diastolic blood pressure (the lowest pressure in the arteries between two heartbeats).

If these numbers increase to 120-139/80-89 mm Hg, this is considered "Prehypertension". If steps are not taken to manage it, people with prehypertension are likely to develop high blood pressure. Having levels of blood pressure 140/90 mm Hg and above is classified as "Hypertension". At this stage, doctors usually recommend lifestyle changes and may prescribe blood pressure medication.

The Dietary Approaches to Stop Hypertension (DASH) was one of the first of the studies conducted by the National Heart, Lung, and Blood Institute (NHLBI) to determine the possible effect of overall diet in safeguarding against high blood pressure.

In this study, 459 adults with levels of systolic blood pressure less than 160 mm Hg and diastolic blood pressure of 80-95 mmHg participated. Around 27% of these had high blood pressure.

The participants were divided into three groups where each followed a different eating plan. The first diet plan composed of foods consumed by most Americans. The second had increased amounts of intake of fruits and vegetables. Third was the DASH diet.

Results showed that the participants following the latter two diets, the one containing more intake of fruits and vegetables and the DASH diet, managed to lower their blood pressure. Be that as it may, it is important to note that the DASH diet produced the finest results. Participants managed to lower the levels of their blood pressure within two weeks.

CHAPTER 3

Dietary Approaches to Stop Hypertension

Learn how to prevent high blood pressure and improve your overall health. This diet places the emphasis on eating a big variety of food, in the correct portions, while also getting all the nutrients your body needs.

Primarily the DASH diet helps to reduce your sodium intake, and thus treat or prevent higher blood pressure. Secondly, consuming such a variety of nutritious foods, mainly fruits and vegetables, full of magnesium, potassium, and calcium also helps to lower hypertension.

In order for any balanced diet to be effective, it needs to become a lifestyle, a lifelong attitude to healthier eating habits. This is exactly what this DASH diet wants you to do. In merely two weeks you may lower hypertension by some points and in the long run it is possible to reduce the count by even eight to fourteen points. This undoubtedly will considerably lower your health hazards.

Last but not least, the DASH diet offers additional benefits like the prevention of strokes, diabetes, cancer, osteoporosis and heart disease because it constitutes a healthy, balanced diet, according to dietary recommendations.

DASH Diet and Sodium Levels

The average American sodium intake comes to a staggering 3400 mg a day while the recommended amount is less than 2300 mg, according to the Dietary Guidelines. The Heart Association's daily recommendation is 1500 mg at most for adults. That is why the DASH diet offers two versions to choose from, according to your specific health needs:

- **The Standard DASH Diet:** Daily intake of sodium of no more than 2300 mg.
- **The Lower Sodium DASH Diet:** Daily sodium intake of less than 1500 mg.

Both of the above versions includes plenty of vegetables and fruits, low-fat and fat-free dairy products, as well as whole grains, poultry, fish and seeds and nuts in moderation. Also included are sweets, meats and oils and fat in lesser amounts.

DASH Diet and Which Foods to Eat

In a nutshell: Fruits and vegetables, low-fat or fat-free dairy products, and whole grains should constitute the bulk of your daily intake. You may also include poultry, fish and legumes in smaller amounts and seeds and nuts on a few occasions weekly.

Small amounts of red meat, fats and sweets are allowed now and then. You should stay away from saturated and animal fats, any food high in protein and refined sugars. Your calorie intake should not exceed 2,000 a day.

Recommended Servings

Grains: 6 – 8 servings per day
- Whole-wheat and low-GI and pita bread, brown rice, cereal, oat porridge and whole-wheat pasta.
- One serving constitutes 1 slice of bread and 1 ounce of dry cereal, half a cup of cooked cereal, pasta or rice.
- Whole-wheat grains are a major source of fiber and energy, much more than for example white bread or regular pasta.

- They are also low-fat, so abstain from using butter, cheese or creamy sauces with your grains.

Vegetables: 4 – 5 servings per day
- All vegetables including carrots, tomatoes, potatoes, broccoli, spinach, sweet potatoes, peas and green beans.
- One serving would be 1/2 a cup of cut vegetables, either raw or cooked, and 1 cup of leafy raw green vegetables.
- Vegetables contain fiber and lots of minerals like magnesium, potassium.
- Start thinking of vegetables as a main dish instead of a side.   Serve a medley of vegetables on whole-wheat pasta or brown rice.
- Fresh vegetables are always the first choice, but frozen is also a good option. When you opt for canned vegetables, read the label carefully and choose the low-sodium and no salt added option. Rinse the vegetables well to rid them of excess sodium contained in the liquid.
- Think creatively - when preparing your next stir-fry, replace half the meat with extra vegetables. This will help you to easily reach your recommended daily intake.

Fruits: 4 – 5 servings per day
- All fruits, fresh or dried, like apricots, strawberries, dates, peaches, melon, grape-fruit, raisins, bananas, mangoes etc.
- One serving would consist of a medium sized fruit, ½ a cup of fresh or frozen fruit or about four ounces of fruit juice.
- Almost all fruits are rich in magnesium, potassium and fiber, especially if you leave the

skin on your pears and apples and other fruits with pips. Besides, it adds an extra dash of color to your food.

- Fruit is an easy option; most kinds hardly need any preparation. So, eat it at snack-time, include it in your salads, and round off your meal with a fruit salad with a spoon of fat-free yoghurt and a sprinkling of cinnamon for extra flavor.
- When substituting fresh fruit with canned fruit, read the labels carefully to make sure no extra sugar is added. The same principle goes for fruit juices.
- Some citrus fruits as well as fruit juices for example oranges and grapefruit may affect certain types of medication. Speak to your pharmacist or doctor when prescribed medicine.

Dairy: 2 – 3 servings per day
- Skim milk, low-fat and 2% fat-free milk, low-fat yoghurt, low-fat mozzarella cheese and low-fat cottage cheese.
- One serving measures 1 cup of low-fat milk or yoghurt, and 1 ½ ounces of cheese.
- Dairy is a good source of protein, calcium and vitamin D, but make sure you stick to the fat-free or low-fat options since dairy products also contain quite a bit of saturated fats.
- If you suffer from digestive problems, select lactose-free products.
- Fat-free or even low-fat frozen yoghurt makes a nice sweet treat on a hot summer's day. Add plenty of fruit for your light lunch.
- Remember that many cheeses, even low-fat ones contain sodium, so stick to the recommended servings.

Lean meat, fish and poultry: 6 servings or less per day

- All kinds of fish without the skin, lean meat with all the fat removed, poultry without the skin.
- Heart-friendly fish like salmon, tuna or herring contain omega-3 acids and will help to lower cholesterol.
- One portion of the above mentioned should not weigh more than six ounces.
- Meat is a good source of protein, magnesium and iron, zinc and vitamins, all of which your body needs.
- Prepare your meat by baking, broiling, roasting or grilling it. Avoid fried products as far as possible.
- Eating smaller portions of meat will allow you to eat more vegetables and fruit to reach your daily recommended serving.

Legumes, seeds and nuts: 4 – 5 servings per week

- Nuts like macadamia, walnuts, almonds, peanuts, sunflower seeds, pumpkin seeds, chickpeas, kidney beans and lentils.
- Food in this category should be eaten only occasionally and in small portions because they have a high calorie count. Therefore, a serving comes to 1/3 of a cup of nuts, 1/2 a cup of cooked beans and lentils and about 2 tablespoons of seeds.
- Foods in this family are a good source of potassium, magnesium and fiber. Additionally, they contain phytochemicals, a chemical compound naturally found in plants, which may reduce the instance of heart disease and cancer.
- Nuts are notorious for a high fat content, but luckily it is the healthier kind of fat like mono-unsaturated and omega-3 acids. Nevertheless, you should stick to the suggested smaller servings.
- To avoid overindulging, rather than consuming them on their own, add your portion of nuts to your breakfast cereal, salads or stir-fries.
- Substitute meat with soybean products like tofu, or tempeh which contain all the amino acids our bodies need to make complete proteins.

Oils and fats: 2 – 3 servings per day

- Soft margarine, unsaturated fats like canola oil, sunflower and olive oil.
- One serving of fat or oil consists of 1 teaspoon of soft margarine and 1 tablespoon of the oils.
- Our bodies need fat in order to absorb some essential vitamins. It also boosts the immune system. However, too much can be detrimental to your heart and may cause obesity and

diabetes. It is therefore essential to limit fat intake to 30% of the daily calorie count.

- Items like crackers, snack food and packaged baked goods contain trans fats, one of the major enemies in increasing the risks of cholesterol and other artery diseases. Trans fats are made through the chemical process of hydrogenation to increase the shelf life of oils and other products.
- Instead of bought salad dressing, sprinkle your salad with a few drops of olive oil and lemon juice. If you prefer readymade salad dressings, avoid those which contain trans fats and saturated fat.
- Always examine food labels to make sure you know which kind of fats and oils they contain. Saturated fats are present in meat, cheese, butter, eggs and cream amongst others.

Sweets: 5 serving or less per week

- Sorbets, fruit ices, hard candy, low-fat cookies.
- Just because you are following the DASH diet does not mean that you have to pull your sweet tooth completely. You are allowed to eat sweets, but in very small quantities. Choose your sweets well and do not think that if you substitute your normal cola for a diet soda, you can drink the same quantity as previously. The sugar content is still much higher than what this diet recommends.
- To help satisfy that sweet tooth, use artificial sweeteners for example NutraSweet and Equal. Even so, go easy on them.
- Refrain from adding extra sugar to your food for instance fruit like strawberries and grapefruit. Most fruit and fruit juices already has a high sugar content. You will learn to appreciate the

authentic flavor of the fruit itself without any added sugar, it only piles up the calorie count.

Alcohol, Caffeine and the DASH Diet

The DASH diet allows alcohol consumption, but in moderation. The recommended quantities are one glass per day for women and two glasses per day for men. This however does not mean that you can skip a day or two and drink six glasses on the third day. Binge drinking is dangerous and may cause harm to the liver, brain and heart. It also elevates blood pressure within a short period of time.

We all know that caffeine may increase the blood pressure, although temporarily. However, any influence caffeine has on hypertension remains inconclusive. Listen to your body. If you are already suffering from high blood pressure, and suspect that caffeine intake increases your hypertension, it is best to avoid it altogether and consult your doctor.

Weight Loss and the DASH Diet

Because the DASH diet subscribes a healthy, balanced diet program, in time you just may find yourself a few pounds lighter. Cutting out added sugars, processed foods, refined grains, saturated fats and oils, consuming less meat and more vegetables and fruit, will most probably make for a slimmer, healthier you.

An improved metabolism may also help you in this regard. This diet allows 2000 calories per day so if you are adamant to lose more weight, cut down on the calorie count, taking your age, body frame and length into account.

How do I reduce my sodium levels?

- By adhering to the DASH diet, you are already doing so. Most of the foods which make up this diet contain little or no sodium.

- Processed foods are the main culprits. Your favorite turkey or ham slices, canned vegetables, and many ready-made dishes contain far too much sodium. Make sure to read the food labels carefully.

- If you are used to a lot of salt; without it, food might taste bland and flavorless, begin to cut back gradually. Add more herbs and spices to your food to enhance the flavor. A teaspoon of salt contains 2325 mg of sodium, so try to banish the salt shaker from your dining table eventually.

- Do not become impatient; remember that it may take up to a few weeks until your taste buds fully adjust to lower salt meals.

Finally: The Right Approach

You are probably about to make profound changes to your eating habits, so take it one step at a time. Rome was not built in a day! If you are not used to eating so much fruit and vegetables, start by adding an extra fruit as a snack or desert each day. Gradually introduce whole-wheat grains by mixing it with your usual pasta or cereal. If your previous diet did not contain a lot of fiber, introduce it slowly to prevent a bloated feeling or upset stomach.

- In order for any balanced diet to be effective, it needs to become a lifestyle, a lifelong approach to healthy eating habits. Remind yourself that you are embarking on a new, healthier way of life because this is exactly what the DASH diet does.

- Stay positive should you occasionally fall short; you are only human. Do not dwell on your mishaps; rather try to find the cause, forgive yourself and carry on with your DASH diet plan.

- Reward yourself on a regular basis – not with sweets or food items, but by going to the theater, watching a movie with an old friend or reading your favorite book in bed on a Sunday morning.

- Take up some form of physical activity. Start walking more, take up cycling or join a dancing group. You will feel more inspired to continue on your new way of life. It will also help you to relax you and thus reduce your hypertension even more.

- If you are fighting an uphill battle and feel that you are not progressing much; seek help. Ask a friend or partner to support you in your endeavors and if that does not help, consult a dietician or your doctor.

- Remember, eating a healthy, balanced diet does not take the fun out of food! The DASH diet offers such a huge variety of choices that you will never become bored with your menu. Be creative and experiment with different combinations of food. There is a wide range of DASH recipes in this book to help you get started.

- Above all, on this DASH diet, your body is now receiving all the nutrients it needs to keep you healthy.

CHAPTER 4

Foods that Lower Your Blood Pressure

It is a well-known fact that the popular DASH Diet can be instrumental in preventing or normalizing blood pressure which is too high. This diet contains foods with low sodium content as well as those rich in calcium, potassium and magnesium. But what if you prefer specific foods instead of supplements? Which foods can you concentrate on to have the same beneficial effects? Research provides the following answers.

Dairy

In 2012 Australian researchers published an article in the Human Hypertension Journal. In this article, they show that their research found a definite link between a lower hypertension risk and the intake of dairy products low in fat content. A diet of low-fat milk and yoghurt was found to be especially effective while low-fat cheese did not seem to have the same benefits. During digestion, peptides and other compounds are released and these, more than the calcium in low-fat dairies, are probably the main life-savers which protect you from hypertension. It is not yet clear why dairy high in fat do not help to protect you from high blood pressure but the assumption is that the culprit may be the saturated fats. It may also simply be the fact that people who prefer low-fat products are more health conscious and therefore lead a healthier lifestyle.

Flaxseed

In 2013 a six-month long study was carried out to determine the effects of the consumption of flaxseed in various foods on patients suffering from hypertension. Both types of blood pressure, namely diastolic and systolic were measured. (The latter is during heart contractions and the former when it relaxes.) Even participants on medication for high blood pressure benefited from flaxseed. Flaxseed contains alpha -linolenic acid (an omega-3 fatty acid), peptides, fiber and lignans and it is assumed that these compounds are responsible for a reduction in blood pressure.

Chocolate

In 2010 a meta-analysis published in BMC Medicine showed that foods rich in flavanols like dark chocolate and cocoa can be linked to the reduction of both types of blood pressure. This occurred in people suffering from hypertension as well as pre-hypertension participants. Blood pressure lowers when blood vessels expand and blood-flow is eased. Nitric oxide helps to do just this. According to another study, polyphenols and especially flavanols, found in products with cocoa, produce the manufacturing of the nitric oxide your body needs to widen arteries. The researchers stated that more research is necessary to determine the role genetics play.

Olive Oil

In 2012 a study was conducted by Spanish researchers over a four months' time frame. The purpose of their research was to compare the benefits, if any, of the intake of olive oil rich in polyphenol versus oils without polyphenol. The study was done on young women who suffer from mild hypertension. Their results conclusively showed that a drop in both diastolic and systolic blood pressure occurred. The higher the blood pressure, the more effective the reduction in blood pressure was found to be.

Beets

Australian researchers were curious to determine whether the consumption of beets could have any effects on hypertension. For the study, they selected participants of both sexes. During the study, conducted in 2013 and published in the Journal for Nutrition, the participants were given either a mixture of apple and beet juice, or just apple juice to drink while the blood pressure counts were monitored and recorded over a 24-hour period. The results were interesting: Six or seven hours after their beet juice intake, participants' systolic blood pressure was reduced. This was especially found amongst the male participants.

Pistachios

A study to look at the effects of pistachios on hypertension was not altogether conclusive but provides some guidelines. This research was done in 2013 and published in a Hypertension Journal. All the volunteers suffered from low density lipoprotein hypertension. They were given either a single serving of these nuts per day or a daily two servings. The lower intake of pistachios proved to be better at lowering their blood pressure. It is however not clear whether this effect was achieved because a higher blood volume was pumped through the heart.

Pomegranate

The possible benefit of the juice of pomegranates on high blood pressure was the object of a study done in England and subsequently published in Human Nutrition and Plant Foods. Both middle-aged and young people were included in this study. They were given a cup or more of juice each day over a four-week period. The result was a reduction in both kinds of hypertension and the deduction is made that it might be due to the polyphenols and potassium in pomegranates.

Fatty Fish

A number of researchers from Portugal, Spain, Ireland and Iceland worked on a study to look into the benefits of diets rich in fish on people who are obese or overweight and who are on a of diet, trying to lose weight. Participants had to eat fatty fish for example salmon, three times every week. (Lean fish like cod was not included in the diet.) After a period of eight weeks they found reductions in the participants' level of blood pressure. This confirmed the results of a number of previous studies. They all conclude that the omega-3 fatty acids which are naturally found in fatty fish are conducive to a reduction in blood pressure.

Whole Grains

In 2012, The American Clinical Nutrition Journal published a research paper done by British researchers. This paper looks at the differences between a refined grain diet and a whole-wheat diet. (In the last instance, oats were combined with whole grains.) The group of middle-aged participants all presented with a lower instance of systolic blood pressure when consuming three helpings of the whole grains. The researchers could not explain the reason for this, but many previous studies have shown how beneficial a whole grain diet is for someone with high cholesterol.

Hibiscus

During this study, done in 2010 at the Tufts University, researchers from Jean Mayer United States Department of Agriculture wanted to delve into the effects which hibiscus tea could have on people suffering from pre-hypertension and mild hypertension. The Research Center of Human Nutrition on Aging conducted the study. Over a period of a month and a half, subjects were asked to drink three cups of this tea daily. The results showed conclusively how diastolic and systolic blood pressure was reduced, more pronouncedly in those subjects with an initially higher systolic hypertension. The effect may be explained by the high concentration of antioxidants like anthocyanins and phenols which are found in hibiscus tea.

CHAPTER 5

DASH Diet Recipes – Main Meals

BREAKFAST

Buckwheat Pancakes

Dietitian's tip:
You may decide to top the pancakes with sliced fresh fruits instead of using maple syrup. Suitable fruits include peaches, bananas and strawberries.

Serves 6

Ingredients
- 2 egg whites
- 1 tablespoon canola oil
- 1/2 cup fat-free milk
- 1/2 cup all-purpose (plain) flour
- 1/2 cup buckwheat flour
- 1 tablespoon baking powder
- 1 tablespoon sugar
- 1/2 cup sparkling water
- 3 cups sliced fresh strawberries

Preparation:
- Whisk the canola oil, egg whites and milk together in a bowl.
- Measure the sugar, baking powder as well as the flours into a separate, larger bowl. Add sparkling water, then the oil mixture, stirring until it is slightly moistened.
- Put a griddle or nonstick pan on medium heat. The pan will be warm enough when a water drop sizzles when dropped into the pan. Carefully spoon half a cup of the pancake mixture into the warm pan. Tilt the pan to spread the batter evenly over the surface of your pan.
- When the top of your pancake forms bubbles and turns slightly brown along the edges (around 2 minutes) and then turn the pancake over. In another minute or so the bottom should start to brown and your pancake is done.
- Place pancakes onto individual plates, spread half a cup of the sliced strawberries over the pancake and serve.

Nutrition Information:
Serving size: 1 pancake
Per Serving:
Total carbohydrate 24 g, Dietary fiber 3 g, Sodium 150 mg, Saturated fat trace, Total fat 3 g, Cholesterol trace, Protein 5 g, Monounsaturated fat 2 g, Calories 143

Peanut Butter & Banana Breakfast Smoothie

Dietitian's Tip:
This extremely simple breakfast is a DASH Diet dream due to the banana and non-fat milk providing lots of potassium.

Serves 1

Ingredients:
- 1 cup nonfat milk

- 1 tablespoon all natural peanut butter
- 1 medium banana, frozen or fresh

Preparation:
- Pour the milk into a blender. Add the rest of the ingredients. Blend until smooth enough.

Nutrition Information:
Per Serving:
Calories 285, Total fat 8.4 g, Saturated fat 1 g, Carbohydrates 42 g, Protein 13 g, Fiber 4 g, Sodium 186 mg, Potassium 882 mg, Magnesium 32 mg, Calcium 506 mg

Cinnamon French Toast

Dietitian's tip:
This low-fat version of the French toast uses cinnamon bread. Any other type of bread would also work as well. Just dip the bread in the egg-milk mixture before frying it.

Serves 2

Ingredients:
- 4 egg whites
- 1 teaspoon vanilla
- 1/8 teaspoon ground nutmeg
- 4 slices cinnamon bread
- 1/4 teaspoon ground cinnamon
- 1/4 cup maple syrup

Preparation:

- Place the nutmeg, vanilla and egg whites in a shallow bowl and whisk until mixed well. Dip each slice of bread in the eggs, making sure to cover all surfaces.
- Heat a griddle or nonstick pan until moderately warm. The pan is ready when a water drop sizzles when placed into it. Place a slice of bread in the pan and sprinkle with a pinch of cinnamon. Flip the bread over and cook for another four or five minutes until golden brown.
- Place the French toasts on individual, slightly heated plates. Using a small sieve, sprinkle one teaspoon of powdered sugar over each slice, followed by two tablespoons of maple syrup and serve.

Nutritional Information:

Serving size: 2 slices
Per Serving:
Total fat 3 g, Calories 299, Protein 11 g, Cholesterol 0 mg, Total carbohydrate 57 g, Dietary fiber < 1 g, Monounsaturated fatTrace, Saturated fatTrace, trans fat 0 g, Sodium 334 mg, Added sugars 17 g

Refrigerator Overnight Oatmeal

Dietitian's Tip:
This is almost a perfect breakfast recipe as its high fiber and tasty. It should do the job of ensuring you are full the whole morning. The yogurt and milk provide the oats with lots of moisture that soften them up. You may even like to sometimes add a tablespoon of cocoa powder. Doing this will make your oatmeal even more interesting with chocolate flavor.

Serves 2

Ingredients:
- 1 cup old fashion oatmeal, uncooked
- 1 cup non-fat vanilla yogurt
- ½ cup non-fat milk
- 1 cup frozen blueberries
- 1 Tablespoon chia seeds

Preparation:
- In a bowl, mix all the ingredients well.
- Divide the mixture into 2 and store in individual containers with airtight lids.
- Keep in the fridge overnight and treat yourself to a fresh oatmeal breakfast in the following morning.

Nutrition Information:
Per Serving:
Calories 370, Total fat 5 g, Saturated fat 1 g, Carbohydrate 66 g, Protein 16 g, Fiber 12 g, Sodium 5 mg, Potassium 258 mg, Magnesium 5 mg, Calcium 274 mg

Sweet Millet Congee

Dietitian's Tip:
Congee is a type of porridge popular in parts of Asia. This whole grain breakfast is made with millet or rice and is a great make-ahead kind of meal. You can prepare a batch during the weekend. Then portion them into several single servings using microwave-safe containers and keep in the fridge. You now have a healthy meal of breakfast ready for the next several days. All that is required is to heat it up each morning.

Serves 8

Ingredients:
- 8 strips of bacon
- 1 cup hulled millet
- 5 cups water
- 1 cup sweet potato, peeled and diced
- 2 teaspoons ginger, minced (optional)
- 1 teaspoon ground cinnamon
- 2 Tablespoons brown sugar
- 1 medium apple, diced with skin
- ¼ cup honey

Preparation:
- Over medium heat, cook the bacon in your pan until crispy. Place in a dish and remove all excess fat by blotting with paper towels. As soon as it has cooled, break the bacon strips into pieces.
- Rinse the millet well and drain.
- Measure the water, millet, ginger, sweet potato, brown sugar and cinnamon into a large pot. As

soon as it starts to boil, lower the heat and allow it to simmer until the water has been absorbed. This will take about one hour. The millet should be cooked.

- Remove the pot from the heat. Now add the honey, bacon bits and apple.
- If using a slow cooker, reduce the water to only four cups and cook for between two and 2 1/2 hours on high.

Nutrition Information:

Per Serving:
Calories 210, Total fat 4 g, Saturated fat 1 g, Carbohydrate 37 g, Protein 7 g, Fiber 5 g, Sodium 207 mg, Potassium 189 mg, Magnesium 12 mg, Calcium 19 mg

LUNCH

<u>Fresh Shrimp Spring Rolls</u>

Dietitian's Tip:
Freshly made spring rolls are a healthy and recommended alternative to those that are deep fried. Adding herbs, vegetables and shrimp give this highly protein packed lunch lots of flavor. Be creative and experiment with different herbs and vegetables.

Serves 6 – (2 spring rolls per serving)

Ingredients:
- 12 sheets of rice paper
- 12 bib lettuce leaves
- 12 basil leaves
- ¾ cup fresh cilantro
- 1 cup carrots, shredded
- ½ medium cucumber, thinly sliced

- 1 ¼ pounds (20 ounces) shrimp, cooked, de-veined and peeled

Preparation:
- Thoroughly wash the basil, lettuce, cilantro, cucumber and carrots. Dry and prepare.
- On a counter, line up all the vegetables in the order in which you are going to use them, like an assembly line.
- On a cleaned surface or cutting board, place a damp kitchen paper towel. Under lukewarm water, wet a sheet of the rice paper and place it on the paper towel.
- Starting on your end of the sheet of rice paper, layer a lettuce leaf, a tablespoon of cilantro, a basil leaf, some cucumber and carrots. Carefully start to roll your rice paper sheet over your vegetables, similar to rolling a burrito. As soon as the vegetables are all covered, add four shrimp and continue the rolling process. Similar to a burrito, make sure to tuck the ends in to prevent the filling from falling out.
- Repeat this process for all the rolls. Serve and enjoy.

Nutrition Information:
Per Serving:
Calories 180, Total fat 2 g, Saturated fat 0 g, Carbohydrate 17 g, Protein 22 g, Fiber 1 g, Sodium 173 mg, Potassium 270 mg, Magnesium 40 mg, Calcium 67 mg

Mayo-less Tuna Salad

Dietitian's Tip:

To ensure that this recipe meets the DASH diet approved requirement, use tuna having not more than 200mg sodium per serving. Experiment with different pasta's shapes including shells and bowtie. To make this an even more well-balanced meal, consider serving with a glass of milk, a piece of fruit, or a low-sodium soup.

Serves 2

Ingredients:

- 5 oz can light tuna in water, drained
- 1 tablespoon extra-virgin olive oil
- 1 tablespoon red wine vinegar
- ¼ cup chopped green onion tops
- 2 cups arugula
- 1 cup cooked pasta (from 2 oz dry)
- 1 tablespoon fresh shaved parmesan cheese
- black pepper

Preparation:

- Using a large mixing bowl, toss the onion tops, tuna, olive oil, arugula, vinegar, as well as the cooked pasta of your choice. Mix carefully.
- Dish up onto two plates, sprinkle with pepper and parmesan and enjoy.

Nutrition Information:

Per Serving:
Calories 245, Total fat 7 g, Saturated fat 1.3 g, Carbohydrates 23 g, Protein 23 g, Fiber 1 g, Sodium 290 mg, Potassium 305 g, Magnesium 46 g, Calcium 85 mg

Baked Oatmeal

Dietitian's tip:
This is another one of those meals that can easily be prepared ahead. Just do the mixing in the evening and leave it in the fridge overnight. When you want to eat, simply put it in the oven and the meal will be ready within minutes. It is healthily suitable as a DASH diet.

Serves 8

Ingredients:
- 1 tablespoon canola oil
- 1/2 cup unsweetened applesauce
- 1/3 cup brown sugar
- Egg substitute equivalent to 2 eggs, or 4 egg whites
- 3 cups uncooked rolled oats
- 2 teaspoons baking powder
- 1 teaspoon cinnamon
- 1 cup skim milk

Preparation:
- Set the oven for 350 degrees F.
- In a large mixing bowl, measure the oil, eggs, sugar and applesauce. Then add all the dry ingredients followed by the milk and mix thoroughly.
- Using cooking spray, generously spray a nine by thirteen-inch baking pan.
- Spoon the mixture into your baking pan and place in the oven.
- Bake uncovered for around half an hour.

Nutrition Information:
Serving size: About 3/4 cup

Per Serving:
Total carbohydrate 33 g, Dietary fiber 3 g, Sodium
105 mg, Saturated fat 0.5 g, Total fat 4 g, Cholesterol
0.5 mg, Protein 7 g, Monounsaturated fat 2 g, Calories
196, Trans fat 0 g, Added sugars 8.5 g

Beef Stroganoff

Dietitian's tip:
There are a few alternatives to using egg noodles for
this recipe. One is replacing the noodles with rice.

Serves 4

Ingredients:
- 1/2 cup chopped onion

- 1/2 pound boneless beef round steak, cut 3/4-inch thick, all fat removed
- 4 cups uncooked yolkless egg noodles
- 1/2 can fat-free cream of mushroom soup (undiluted)
- 1/2 cup of water
- 1 tablespoon all-purpose (plain) flour
- 1/2 teaspoon paprika
- 1/2 cup fat-free sour cream

Preparation:
- Over medium heat, sauté onions in your nonstick pan until translucent. This will take about five minutes. Now add your beef strips. Continue cooking until the strips are tender and cooked through.
- Drain on paper towels and leave aside.
- Using a large sized pot, boil enough water to fill ¾ of the pot. Add noodles to the boiling water and cook for about 12 minutes until tender (al dente). Drain pasta thoroughly.
- Over a medium heat, mix together the flour, soup and water in a medium sized saucepan. Stir constantly until your sauce has thickened. Pour the sauce into the pan with the beef. Add the paprika and stir until everything is heated through.
- Remove the pan from the heat and stir in sour cream.
- Spoon pasta onto individual plates, cover with the stroganoff and serve.

Nutrition Information:
Serving size: About 2 1/2 cups
Per Serving:

Calories 273, Total fat 5 g, Saturated fat 2 g, Trans fat Trace 0 g, Monounsaturated fat 2 g, Cholesterol 82 mg, Sodium 193 mg, Total carbohydrate 37 g, Dietary fiber 2 g, Added sugars 0 g, Protein 20 g

Salmon Salad Pita

Dietitian's Tip:
This serving of salad provides plenty of very desirable omega-3 oils. It could be further enhanced when serve with lemon wedges and fat-free yogurt used as replacement for the tartar sauce. Crackers or whole grain bread could also be as a healthy substitute for the pita.

Serves 3

Ingredients:
- ¾ cup canned Alaskan salmon
- 3 tablespoons plain fat-free yogurt
- 1 tablespoon lemon juice
- 2 tablespoons red bell pepper, minced
- 1 tablespoon red onion, minced
- 1 teaspoon capers, rinsed and chopped
- Pinch of dill, fresh or dried
- Black pepper to taste
- 3 lettuce leaves
- 3 pieces' small whole wheat pita bread

Preparation:
- Gently mix together the first eight ingredients in a bowl.

- Spread a lettuce leaf on the pita, and spoon about a third cup of the salmon salad into each pita.
- Serve and enjoy.

Nutrition Information:

Per Serving:

Calories 180, Total fat 4 g, Saturated fat 0.5 g, Carbohydrates 19 g, Protein 19 g, Fiber 3 g, Sodium 420 mg, Potassium 331 mg, Magnesium 43 mg, Calcium 60 mg

DINNER

Chicken and Broccoli Stir Fry

Dietitian's Tip:
To derive maximum nutrients from the meal, use 100% orange juice. This will help limit the added sugar and be an even better DASH diet recipe. Include a glass of non-fat milk will provide additional nutrient and make a truly well-rounded meal. If desire, consider adding zucchini and peppers for the antioxidants.

Serves 4

Ingredients:
- 1/3 cup orange juice
- 1 Tbsp low-sodium soy sauce
- 1 Tbsp Schezuan sauce
- 2 tsp cornstarch

- 1 Tbsp canola oil
- 1 lb boneless chicken breast, cut into 1 inch cubes
- 2 cups of frozen broccoli florets
- 1 6-oz package of frozen snow peas
- 2 cups shredded cabbage
- 2 cups of cooked brown rice
- 1 Tbsp sesame seeds (optional)

Preparation:
- In a small mixing bowl, mix the two sauces and the orange juice with the cornstarch.
- Heat the oil in the wok, then add the chicken strips and stir fry until done, around five to seven minutes.
- Add broccoli, cabbages and snow peas and the juice and sauce mixture. Cook everything for abound five minutes until warmed through.
- Dish up over the brown rice. If using, sprinkle some sesame seeds on top.

Nutrition Information:
Per Serving:
Calories 340, Total fat 8 g, Saturated fat 2 g, Carbohydrate 35 g, Protein 28 g, Fiber 5 g, Sodium 240 mg, Calcium 80 mg

Broccoli and Cheese Stuffed Chicken

Dietitian's Tip:
Use frozen broccoli florets if you are short of time. In terms of nutrients, frozen vegetables generally have just as much as fresh ones. Pile the chicken on top of some quinoa or brown rice to compete the entrée.

Serves 9

Ingredients:
- 3 (8 oz. each) large chicken breasts
- 1 large egg
- 2 teaspoon water
- ¾ cup whole wheat seasoned bread crumbs
- 2 cups broccoli florets, cooked, chopped small
- 5 slices reduced fat Swiss cheese (3/4 oz. per slice)
- Spray oil
- Toothpicks

Preparation:
- Heat the oven, set at 350 degrees F.
- In a smallish bowl, beat the water and egg together using a fork.
- Spoon the breadcrumbs into another shallow bowl.
- Now slice each chicken breast fillet into three thin cutlets. To make the cutlets even thinner, pound carefully. This makes them easier to wrap.
- Cut the cheese slices in half. Put one halved slice in the middle of the cutlet. Cover the cheese with some of the broccoli. Now wrap the cutlet around the filling and secure with toothpicks.

- Dip the chicken parcel in the egg wash and then cover with breadcrumbs.
- Spray a cookie pan with oil, then place the chicken parcels onto the sheet. Spray each chicken parcel with canola oil; then bake for around 25 minutes, or until cooked.

Nutrition Information:

Per Serving:
Kcal 150, Total fat 4 g, Saturated fat 1.5 g, Carbohydrates 7 g, Protein 20 g, Fiber 1 g, Sodium 280 mg, Potassium 330 mg, Magnesium 24 mg, Calcium 152 mg

Beef Stew

Dietitian's tip:

This is one of those DASH diet meals that comes with lots of meat. But it is nevertheless full of vegetables and flavor.

Serves 4

Ingredients:
- 1 pound beef round steak
- 2 teaspoons canola oil
- 2 cups diced yellow onions
- 1 cup diced celery
- 1 cup diced Roma tomatoes
- 1/2 cup diced sweet potato
- 1/2 cup diced white potato with skin
- 1/2 cup diced mushrooms
- 1 cup diced carrot
- 4 cloves of garlic, chopped
- 1 cup chopped kale
- 1/4 cup uncooked barley
- 1/4 cup red wine vinegar
- 1 teaspoon balsamic vinegar
- 3 cups low-sodium vegetable or beef stock
- 1 teaspoon dried sage, crushed
- 1 teaspoon minced fresh thyme
- 1 tablespoon minced fresh parsley
- 1 tablespoon dried oregano
- 1 teaspoon dried rosemary, minced
- black pepper, to taste

Preparation:
- Heat a grill or a broiler to medium heat. Broil or grill the steaks for about six minutes, turn and repeat for another six minutes on the other side. Make sure not to overcook them. Set aside.
- Using a large sized stock pot, fry all the vegetables over a medium heat, stirring constantly. They should be light brown, about ten minutes. Add the barley; then cook for another five minutes.

- Using paper towels, pat the steak dry and cut into small pieces. Now add to the pot with the herbs, spices, stock and vinegars.
- Simmer for about one hour until the stew is thick and the barley cooked.

Nutrition Information:
Serving size: About 2 cups
Per Serving:
Total carbohydrate 35 g, Dietary fiber 7 g, Sodium 166 mg, Saturated fat 2 g, Total fat 9 g, Trans fat 0 g, Cholesterol 84 mg, Protein 42 g, Monounsaturated fat 4 g, Calories 389, Added sugars 0 g

Asian Beef and Noodles

Dietitian's Tip:
With this recipe of ramen noodles, you get plenty of protein with ground-beef. You also get to pick your choice of vegetables to help make this into a very tasty main dish. Serve with some fruits and if desired, a glass of milk. This will make a complete meal.

Serves 6

Ingredients:
- 2 cups water
- 1/2 pound lean ground beef (15% fat)
- 2 packages oriental flavor instant ramen-style noodles, broken into small pieces
- 1 seasoning packet from ramen-style noodles (save other packet for another use)

- 16 ounces frozen Asian-style vegetables, or any other frozen vegetables
- 2 green onions, thinly sliced
- 1 tablespoon fresh ginger or 1/4 teaspoon ground ginger
- 2 cloves garlic, minced, or 1/2 teaspoon garlic powder

Preparation:
- Brown the ground beef over medium heat in a large skillet. (If using an electric one, set at 350 degrees F). When it is cooked through, drain the fat.
- Add only one of the seasoning packets and two cups water and mix everything well.
- Add the green onion, garlic, ginger and frozen vegetables. Adjust the heat to bring to boiling point.
- As soon as the mixture is boiling, add the ramen noodles and immediately lower the heat to simmer for about three to five minutes. Stir occasionally.
- Any leftovers may be frozen as soon as it has cooled to room temperature.

Nutrition Information:
Serving size = 1 cup
Per Serving:
Calories 270, Total fat 10 g, Saturated fat 4 g, Carbohydrates 27 g, Protein 17 g, Fiber 3 g, Sodium 486 mg, Potassium 242 mg, Magnesium 19 mg, Calcium 60 mg

Brown Rice Burgers

Dietitian's Tip:
This recipe will be an even better DASH meal with using whole-wheat buns. Add a bit of Dijon mustard, lettuce leaves, sweet onion and sliced tomato. The burgers would be very tasty with grilled fresh asparagus and some olive oil and garlic.

Reduce the portion by half if following the recipe makes too many burgers. Alternatively, excess burgers can be kept in the freezer and be quickly available for another day.

Makes 12 Burgers

Ingredients:
- 2 cups cooked brown rice
- ½ cup parsley, chopped
- 1 cup carrot, finely grated
- ½ cup onion, finely chopped
- 1 clove garlic, minced
- 1 tsp salt
- ¼ tsp ground black pepper
- 2 eggs, beaten
- ½ cup whole wheat flour
- 2 tbsp vegetable oil for cooking

Preparation:
- In a bowl, mix together all the ingredients, except for the oil. Divide the mixture into twelve portions and form into patties.
- Heat the oil in your skillet and cook the patties for about five minutes until they are brown. Flip them over and repeat for another four or five minutes.

Nutrition Information:
Serving size = 1 burger
<u>Per Serving</u>:
Calories 120, Total fat 3.5 g, Saturated fat 0 g,
Carbohydrate 18 g, Protein 3 g, Fiber 3 g, Sodium 150
mg

CHAPTER 6

DASH Diet Recipes – Soups, Salads & Snacks

SOUPS

Gingery Chicken Noodle Soup

Dietitian's tip:
This soup can easily be made vegetarian if needed. Just use vegetable stock and substitute cubes of tofu that are extra-firm for the chicken.

Serves 8

Ingredients:
- 3 ounces dried soba noodles
- 1 tablespoon olive oil
- 1 large yellow onion, chopped
- 1 tablespoon peeled and minced fresh ginger
- 1 carrot, peeled and finely chopped
- 1 clove garlic, minced
- 4 cups chicken stock or broth
- 2 tablespoons reduced-sodium soy sauce
- 1 pound skinless, boneless chicken breasts, chopped
- 1 cup shelled edamame
- 1 cup plain soy milk (soya milk)
- 1/4 cup chopped fresh cilantro (fresh coriander)

Preparation:
- Fill a large saucepan ¾ with water and boil. Add noodles to the pan and cook for around five minutes until al dente. Drain the water and leave aside.
- Use a saucepan to heat the oil over a medium heat. Fry the onion lightly. The onion should be translucent and soft. Add carrots and ginger, then sauté for another minute. Now add garlic, then sauté for thirty seconds more. (The garlic should not turn brown.)
- Add soya sauce as well as the water and turn up the heat until it boils. Add the edamame and chopped chicken. As soon as it starts to boil again, turn the heat down and let it simmer until edamame are soft and the chicken cooked. This will take around four minutes. Lastly add the soy

milk and noodles and gently cook through, it should not boil.

- Remove from heat and add the cilantro. Stir through and, dish up in bowls.

Nutrition Information:

Per Serving:
Calories 184, Total carbohydrate 11 g, Dietary fiber 2 g, Sodium 267 mg, Saturated fat 1 g, Total fat 5 g, Cholesterol 33 mg, Protein 22 g, Monounsaturated fat 2 g

Mushroom Barley Soup

Dietitian's tip:

If you are using precooked barley, you should only add it in after the potato is cooked. This recipe is an excellent opportunity to use up any excess vegetables you have at home. Just add them to the soup.

The sherry may be replaced with extra broth or even be omitted completely.

Serves 9

Ingredients:
- 1 tablespoon canola oil
- 1 1/2 cups chopped onions
- 1 cup sliced mushrooms
- 3/4 cup chopped carrots
- 1 teaspoon dried thyme
- 1/8 teaspoon black pepper
- 1/2 teaspoon chopped garlic
- 8 cups vegetable stock
- 3/4 cup pearl barley
- 3 ounces dry sherry
- 1/2 small potato, chopped
- 1/4 cup thinly sliced green onions

Preparation:
- Heat your oil over medium heat in your stock pot. Add the mushrooms, onions, pepper, garlic and thyme. For about five minutes, sauté until onions are translucent.
- Add the barley and vegetable stock. As soon as the soup starts to boil, turn the heat down and cook for about twenty minutes. When the barley is cooked, stir in the potato and sherry. Cook for another fifteen minutes until the potato is soft.
- Serve with sliced or chopped green onions as garnish.

Nutrition Information:
Serving size: 8 ounces
Per Serving:

Calories 121, Total fat 4 g, Saturated fat 0 g, Trans fat 0 g, Monounsaturated fat 3 g, Cholesterol 0 mg, Sodium 112 mg, Total carbohydrate 19 g, Dietary fiber 3 g, Total sugars 2 g, Protein 2 g

Wild Rice Mushroom Soup

Dietitian's tip:
There is a whole range of mushrooms that will work well with this soup. These include shitake, chanterelle, porcini, portabella, oyster, and cremini. They all have their own unique flavor and about the same calories.

Serves 4

Ingredients:
- 1 tablespoon olive oil
- Half a white onion, chopped
- 1/4 cup chopped celery
- 1/4 cup chopped carrots
- 1 1/2 cups sliced fresh white mushrooms
- 1/2 cup white wine, or 1/2 cup low-sodium, fat-free chicken broth
- 2 1/2 cups low-sodium, fat-free chicken broth
- 1 cup fat-free half-and-half
- 2 tablespoons flour
- 1/4 teaspoon dried thyme
- Black pepper
- 1 cup cooked wild rice

Preparation:
- Place a stock pot over medium heat. Cook the celery, onion and carrots in the heated oil until tender. Now add the white wine, chicken broth and mushrooms. Cover the pot and leave to heat through.
- In a mixing bowl, add the flour, half-and half, pepper and thyme and blend. Add the cooked rice and mix together. Add this to the hot pot with the vegetables, and cook on medium heat until bubbly and thick.
- Serve the soup warmed up.

Nutrition Information:
Serving size: About 1 1/2 cups
Per Serving:
Total carbohydrate 23 g, Dietary fiber 2 g, Sodium 120 mg, Saturated fat 1 g, Total fat 5 g, Cholesterol 3 mg, Protein 8 g, Monounsaturated fat 3 g, Calories 170, Trans fat 0 g, Added sugars 0 g

Summer Vegetable Soup

Dietitian's tip:
This soup can be very flavorful with the many types of herbs and vegetables that are available in summer. Though the list of ingredients in the recipe may appear to be long, the soup can be ready within a short preparation and cooking time.

Serves 8

Ingredients:

- 1 tablespoon olive oil
- 1 yellow onion, chopped (about 1 cup)
- 3 cloves garlic, chopped
- 4 plum (Roma) tomatoes, peeled and seeded, then diced
- 1 tablespoon chopped fresh oregano or 1 teaspoon dried oregano
- 1 teaspoon ground cumin
- 4 cups no salt added vegetable stock or broth
- 1 bay leaf
- 1 carrot, peeled, halved lengthwise, and thinly sliced crosswise (about 1 cup)
- 1 yellow bell pepper, seeded and diced (about 1 cup)
- 1 zucchini, halved lengthwise and thinly sliced crosswise (about 1 cup)
- 1 tablespoon grated lemon zest
- 2 tablespoons chopped fresh cilantro (fresh coriander)
- 1/4 teaspoon salt
- 1/4 teaspoon freshly ground black pepper

Preparation:

- Heat the oil in a saucepan to medium heat. Sauté the onions for about four minutes until translucent and soft. Add garlic, sauté for another thirty seconds - do not let garlic turn brown. Now add the oregano, cumin and tomatoes and cook together until tomatoes are soft, around four minutes.

- Next, add the bay leaf as well as the stock. Heat the soup to boiling point; then lower the heat, allowing the mixture to simmer. Next, add the carrot and bell pepper and let it cook for two minutes. Lastly add zucchini and cook for another three minutes or until all your vegetables are soft.
- Stir in cilantro, lemon zest as well as the seasoning. Remember to discard the bay leaf before dishing up. Serve immediately in individual mugs or bowls.

Nutrition Information:
Serving size: About 1 1/4 cups
Per Serving:
Calories 62, Total fat 2 g, Saturated fat <1 g, Trans fat 0 g, Monounsaturated fat 1 g, Cholesterol 0 mg, Sodium 156 mg, Total carbohydrate 9 g, Dietary fiber 2 g, Total sugars 5 g, Added sugars 0 g, Protein 2 g

Turkey Bean Soup

Dietitian's tip:
Instead of using ground turkey for this soup, you might want to consider using leftover turkey. Either with work equally well.

Serves 4

Ingredients:
- 1 pound ground turkey breast
- 2 medium onions, chopped
- 2 stalks celery, chopped

- 1 clove garlic, minced
- 1/4 cup ketchup
- 1 can (14.5 ounces) unsalted diced tomatoes
- 3 cubes low-sodium chicken bouillon
- 7 cups water
- 1 1/2 teaspoons dried basil
- 1/4 teaspoon ground black pepper
- 2 cups shredded cabbage
- 1 can (15 ounces) unsalted cannellini beans, rinsed and drained

Preparation:
- Using a large enough saucepan to cook the onion, ground turkey, garlic and celery until all the ingredients are soft and cooked through.
- Add the bouillon, ketchup, water, tomatoes, basil, pepper, beans and cabbage.
- First bring to boiling point. Then lower the heat. Cover the saucepan and allow it to simmer for thirty minutes or more.

Nutrition Information:
Serving size: About 3 1/2 cups
Per Serving:
Calories 242, Total fat 2 g, Saturated fat < 1 g, Trans fat 0 g, Monounsaturated fatTrace, Cholesterol 37 mg, Sodium 204 mg, Total carbohydrate 30 g, Dietary fiber 10 g, Added sugars 0 g, Protein 26 g

SALADS

Avocado Egg Salad

Dietitian's Tip:
For best result, boil the eggs in advance and have them chilled. There are different ways to serve this avocado egg salad. It can be on a bed of lettuce, wrapped in whole-wheat tortilla, in a hollowed-out avocado or tomato, or even on a sliced of whole-wheat bread that is toasted. Include a glass of milk if looking for added calcium and magnesium.

Serves 6

Ingredients:
- 4 large hard-boiled eggs, chopped, white and yolk separated
- 4 hard-boiled egg whites, chopped
- 1 medium avocado, cut into ½-inch pieces
- 1 tablespoon light mayonnaise
- 1 tablespoon fat free plain yogurt
- ½ tablespoon finely chopped chives
- 2 teaspoons red wine vinegar
- ½ teaspoon salt
- ¼ teaspoon freshly ground pepper

Preparation:
- Mix together the avocado, egg yolks, chives, yoghurt, salt, pepper and vinegar. Using a fork, mash everything together. Add the egg whites; then mix thoroughly.

Nutrition Information:

<u>Per Serving</u>:

Calories 114, Total fat 8 g, Saturated fat 2 g, Carbohydrates 4 g, Protein 8 g, Fiber 1 g, Sodium 294 mg, Potassium 192 mg, Magnesium 6 mg, Calcium 23 mg

<u>Apricot Pasta Salad with Chicken</u>

Dietitian's Tip:

When using fresh apricot, it is recommended that they be kept cool so as to lessen the chances of over-ripening when needed for cooking. The season for fresh apricot tend to be relatively short so it's sometimes not available. For this DASH recipe, it is not critical to only use the fresh ones. Rehydrated dried apricots are fully acceptable.

Serves 4

Ingredients:

For the Dressing
- 2 apricots cut into quarters
- 2 tbsp white wine vinegar
- ¼ tsp salt
- 1 tbsp sugar
- 3 tbsp olive oil
- 1 tbsp finely chopped fresh basil

For the Salad
- ¼ lb fusilli (corkscrew) pasta
- 6 fresh apricots cut into quarters
- 2 cups low sodium chicken broth

- 2 skinless, boneless chicken breasts
- 1 red bell pepper cut into long thin strips
- 2 small zucchini ends trimmed, cut in half then into thin strips
- 1 tbsp chopped fresh basil
- 1 cup apricot basil dressing

Preparation:
- Blend together the vinegar, salt, apricots, and sugar. Keep your bender running and add the oil a little at a time until the mixture is smooth and thick. Switch off your blender and now add the chopped fresh basil. Stir well. It should make one cup.
- Heat chicken broth in a saucepan. Now lower the heat and add the chicken breast fillets. Cover with a lid and simmer for about six minutes, or until the chicken breasts are cooked through. Remove and set aside to cool. Use a fork to shred the chicken into small pieces, bite size would be ideal.
- Cook pasta according to the instructions on the packet, then drain and allow it to cool.
- Mix together the pasta, zucchini, apricots, basil and red pepper in a salad bowl. Lastly, toss the salad with the prepared dressing.
- Serve and enjoy.

Nutrition Information:
Per Serving:
Calories 360, Total fat 15 g, Saturated fat 2.5 g, Carbohydrates 36 g, Protein 11 g, Sodium 230 mg, Fiber 4 g

Creamy Fruit Salad

Dietitian's Tip:
This is a recipe that is bursting with plenty of vitamins, fiber, and minerals. It can be enjoyed as a snack, a dessert, or even as a side dish. A suggestion is to serve it together with a glass of milk and a toast with perhaps peanut butter.

Serves 8

Ingredients:
- 1 cup pineapple chunks
- 1 large apple, chopped
- 1 banana, sliced
- 1 orange, chopped
- 3/4 cup low-fat piña colada yogurt (one 6-oz carton of yogurt)

Preparation:
- In a salad bowl, place the pineapple chunks. Then add the bananas, orange and apples pieces.
- Add the yoghurt and mix everything gently. Make sure all the fruit is coated with yoghurt.
- Leftovers should be refrigerated within two hours after preparation.

Notes:
- Try adding different fruits like grapes, blueberries, pears, or peach slices.
- Try different low-fat yogurt flavors like lemon, mango, honey, or vanilla.

Nutrition Information:
Serving size: ½ cup
Per Serving:
Calories 70, Total fat 0 g, Saturated fat 0 g, Carbohydrates 16 g, Protein 1 g, Fiber 2 g, Sodium 15 mg, Potassium 140 mg, Magnesium 10 mg, Calcium 50 mg

Broccoli and Everything Salad

Dietitian's Tip:
Sunflower seeds or sliced grapes may be added to further enhance this salad. Yet another interesting possibility is adding quinoa, a high protein grain, to have a more complete DASH meal. Quinoa is an exceptionally good source of fiber, magnesium, phosphorus, iron, and protein. It also provides the essential amino acids that the body needs.

Serves 8

Ingredients:
- 1 cup raw broccoli, chopped
- 1 medium carrot, peeled and diced
- 2 stalks celery, thinly sliced

- 1/2 cup raisins
- 1/4 cup onion, chopped
- 1 cup cooked ham, chicken or turkey
- 1/4 cup light mayonnaise
- 1/4 cup plain, non-fat yogurt
- 1 tablespoon sugar
- 1 teaspoon vinegar

Preparation:
- Use a large enough bowl to mix together the carrot, broccoli, celery, onion, meat and raisins. In a smaller bowl mix the mayonnaise, sugar, vinegar and yoghurt.
- Now spoon the mayonnaise mixture onto the salad, stirring gently until the meat and vegetables are well covered. Leftovers should be refrigerated within two to three hours after preparation.

Nutrition Information:
Serving size: 2/3 cup
Per Serving:
Calories 110, Total fat 4 g, Saturated fat 1 g, Carbohydrates 14 g, Protein 5 g, Fiber 2 g, Sodium 280 mg, Potassium 279 mg, Magnesium 12 mg, Calcium 32 mg

Mediterranean Tuna Salad

Dietitian's Tip:
This salad can easily be further upgraded to a more complete item simply by including fresh spinach, cherry tomatoes, and seeds.

Serves 10

Ingredients:
- 3 cans (5 ounces each) tuna in water, drained
- 1 cup shredded carrot
- 2 cups diced cucumber
- 1 1/2 cups peas, canned and drained or thawed from frozen
- 3/4 cup low-fat, low-sodium Italian salad dressing

Preparation:
- Put the tuna into a bowl and using a fork, break up the chunks. Add the cucumber, peas, carrot and the dressing. Mix everything well.
- This salad can be made ahead and kept, covered, in the refrigerator until needed.

Nutrition Information:
Per Serving:
Calories 105, Total fat 2 g, Saturated fat 1 g, Carbohydrates 7 g, Protein 14 g, Fiber 2 g, Sodium 241 mg, Potassium 217 mg, Magnesium 26 mg, Calcium 20 mg

SNACKS

Whole Wheat Muffins

Dietitian's Tip:
Enjoy delightful whole-grain muffins for breakfast with yogurt and fruit. They can also be afternoon snack and go well with low-fat milk and nut butter. The muffins carry plenty of fiber, minerals, vitamins and phytochemicals.

Serves 12

Ingredients:
- cooking spray
- 2 cups whole wheat flour
- ½ cup sugar
- 3 ½ teaspoons baking powder
- 2 egg whites
- 3 tablespoons canola oil

- 1 1/3 cups fat-free milk
- 1 tablespoon white vinegar (add this to the non-fat milk and stir well)
- Optional: 1 cup blueberries, fresh or frozen

Preparation:
- Set the oven for 350 degrees Fahrenheit. Spray the muffin tray lightly with the cooking spray. Otherwise use paper liners.
- Combine the flour, baking powder and sugar in a large enough mixing bowl. If you decide to use blueberries, they should be added now to prevent them from dropping to the very bottom.
- Use a separate bowl to combine the remainder of the ingredients. Now add this wet mixture to your dry one. Stir just until everything is moist, make sure not to over-mix.
- Spoon or pour into the muffin tin and bake for 25 to 30 minutes. If the muffin springs back when you touch it, it is ready.

Nutrition Information:
Per Serving:
Calories 146, Total fat 4 g, Saturated fat 0.5 g, Carbohydrates 25 g, Protein 4 g, Fiber 2 g, Sodium 185 mg, Potassium 135 mg, Magnesium 31 mg, Calcium 91 mg

Apple Oat Bran Muffins

Dietitian's Tip:
A suggestion is to bake a batch or two of these muffins for keeping in the freezer. These can be taken out when a quick snack or breakfast is needed. Try to have them individually wrapped before freezing in an air-tight bag or container. They can then be kept for up to a month or so in the freezer.

Serves 12

Ingredients:
- ¾ cups all-purpose flour
- ¾ cups whole wheat flour
- 1 ½ tsp cinnamon
- 1 tsp baking powder
- ½ tsp baking soda
- ¼ tsp salt
- 1 cup buttermilk
- ½ cup oat bran
- ¼ cup firmly packed brown sugar
- 2 tbsp vegetable oil
- 1 large egg
- 1 ½ cups Golden Delicious apples, peeled, cored and finely chopped

Preparation:
- Set the oven for 400 degrees Fahrenheit.
- Grease a dozen muffin cups. You may also use paper liners.
- Mix together both flours, baking powder, cinnamon, salt and baking soda in a bowl.
- Use a separate bowl to beat together the buttermilk, brown sugar, eggs, oil and oat bran.

- When it is well blended, stir this mixture into the flour mixture, do not over-mix. Fold in the apples.
- Spoon into the muffin cups and bake for eighteen to twenty minutes or else until a small knife or wooden pick comes out clean when inserted into the muffins.
- Allow the muffins to cool in the pan for five minutes before turning out. Place on a wire rack to cool completely.

Nutrition Information:
Per Serving:
Calories 121, Total fat 3 g, Protein 4 g, Carbohydrate 21 g, Fiber 3 g, Sodium 134 mg

Potato Nachos

Dietitian's Tip:
In order to save on some calories, fat, and sodium without compromising the flavor, try using lean ground turkey and potatoes in place of nachos. Add a bit of fat-free sour cream before serving.
This recipe can be further improved as a DASH diet by boosting the fiber and potassium content just by replacing the red potatoes with either yams or sweet potatoes. Yams, in particular are great substitute for potatoes or rice in many dishes. They are one of the best sources of vitamins A and C.

Serves 5

Ingredients:

- 1 pound small red potatoes, with skins on
- 2 teaspoons oil or cooking spray
- 8 ounces ground turkey, 99% fat free
- ½ teaspoon chili powder
- ½ cup cheddar cheese, shredded
- 1 cup lettuce, shredded
- 1 medium tomato, diced ¾ cup
- 1 cucumber, peeled and diced
- 1 tablespoon cilantro, chopped
- ¾ cup salsa

Preparation:

- Preheat the oven to 450 degrees Fahrenheit.
- Slice all the potatoes into circles of about a quarter inch thickness. Spray each slice with the cooking spray for three seconds. Otherwise you can coat them lightly with oil.
- Spread them out in one single layer on a large enough baking tray and bake for about half an hour, depending on how brown you want them to be.
- In the meantime, place the chili powder and ground turkey in a skillet. Stirring constantly, cook for about eight to ten minutes until the turkey has browned.
- When the potatoes are done, place them in a casserole or any oven-proof dish. Spoon the turkey over the potatoes, spreading it our evenly. Now sprinkle with the cheese.
- Return the dish to the oven until the cheese has melted; this will take only a few minutes.
- When done, remove from the oven and now top with the tomato, lettuce, cilantro, cucumber and the salsa. Refrigerate any leftovers as soon as the dish has cooled to room temperature.

Nutrition Information:
<u>Per Serving</u>:
Calories 192, Total fat 6 g, Carbohydrates 3 g, Protein 16 g, Fiber 2 g, Sodium 242 mg, Potassium 531 mg, Magnesium 24 mg, Calcium 19 mg

Baked Spinach Artichoke Yogurt Dip

Dietitian's Tip:
One of the key DASH recommendation is having at least 50% of the daily grains whole. This can be easier met when this recipe is served using whole grain toasted bread. An alternative to the bread is reduced-sodium baked crackers.

Serves 8

Ingredients:
- 1 (14-ounce) can artichoke hearts, drained and chopped
- 1 (10-ounce) package frozen chopped spinach, thawed and drained
- 1 (8-ounce) container low-fat plain yogurt or low-fat plain Greek-style yogurt
- 1 cup shredded part-skim, low-moisture Mozzarella cheese
- ¼ cup chopped green onion
- 1 garlic, clove, minced
- 2 tablespoons chopped red pepper

Preparation:
- Heat the oven to a temperature of 350 degrees.
- In a mixing bowl, mix all the ingredients, excluding the red pepper.
- Spoon this mixture into a pie-plate (nine-inch) or a large enough casserole dish. Bake for twenty to twenty-five minutes. After removing it from the oven, sprinkle with the red peppers.
- You can serve the dip with toasted whole grain bread or crackers.

Nutrition Information:
Per Serving:
Calories 90, Total fat 4 g, Saturated fat 2 g, Carbohydrates 8 g, Protein 8 g, Fiber 1 g, Sodium 270 mg, Potassium 129 mg, Magnesium 27 mg, Calcium 197 mg

Crispy Garbanzo Beans

Dietitian's Tip:
Garbanzo beans are a really decent protein source
brimming with extremely important fiber, minerals
and vitamins. They can be mixed with carrot sticks,
low-fat cheese or perhaps whole grain crackers.
Alternatively, for a bit of crunchy surprise, add them
to a salad for an even more healthy meal.

Serves 8

Ingredients:
- 2 cans (15 ounces) unsalted garbanzo beans
- ½ teaspoon salt
- ½ teaspoon pepper
- 1 teaspoon garlic powder or 4 cloves of garlic
- 1 teaspoon onion powder
- 1 teaspoon dried parsley flakes
- 2 teaspoon dried dill
- Cooking spray

Preparation:

- Set the oven at 400 degrees Fahrenheit.
- Drain the garbanzos, then rinse well. Shake the strainer to get rid of all excess water. Now dry them with paper towels. (Wet beans will result in "popping" when heated.)
- Mix the garlic powder, salt, pepper, onion powder, dill and parsley.
- Spray a medium sized rimmed baking pan and spread out the garbanzos on the sheet. Now spray the garbanzo beans also with your cooking spray. Lastly sprinkle the seasoning mixture over, shaking the pan to make sure the seasoning is well distributed. Pat the beans into a single layer.
- Place this sheet onto the very lowest rack of the oven and bake for thirty to forty minutes. Make sure to shake and turn the sheet every ten minutes.
- As soon as the garbanzo beans are golden brown and crispy, they are done.
- Allow to cool and enjoy.

Nutrition Information:

Per Serving:
Calories 111, Total fat 1 g, Saturated fat 0 g, Carbohydrates 20 g, Protein 6 g, Fiber 4 g, Sodium 171 mg, Potassium 222 mg, Magnesium 35 mg, Calcium 51

CONCLUSION

Now that you have read through the entire book on lowering blood pressure naturally through adopting the DASH diet, you would have sufficient idea about what the diet is all about. It's time to have a gradual mindset change and begin eating healthy. Start with a few of the DASH diet recipes found in this book and over time, make eating the right food a way of life. You will see significant benefits within weeks; the most important among these include a reduction of hypertension, weight loss, and a much desirable lifestyle.

Soon after you begin experimenting on the DASH diet, you would very likely find enjoyment and pleasure in eating tastier and more nutritious food. In case you still have doubts on whether you will be able to change your food intake enough to meet the DASH recommendations, do note that there are barely any major restrictions unlike most other diets you might have read about or even attempted in the past. On top of this, the DASH diet is fully flexible so long as you keep in mind that your target is to eat healthy and nutritious food most of the time.

Nevertheless, there could be days or even weeks when you find yourself lacking in discipline and started to eat unhealthy food again. You would then have move away from the DASH diet recommendations but know that you can always stop and reflect on the situation. Then try once more and go for DASH based diet and continue the journey towards the long-term goal. Your occasional setbacks are merely part of the process in striving for the new lifestyle you need and desire. The ultimate destination is where you enjoy a healthy life without the problems of high blood pressure and all its related medical health issues.

When you finally are well on your way towards achieving long-term success with this, you will also have noticed that your blood pressure will no longer be a problem. This may even take place with a few weeks and you will then begin to appreciate that DASH is really a hypertension diet that works.

This book has provided the essential information of what the DASH diet is, the guidelines on the types of food and the correct portions you need, as well as sample DASH diet recipes that you can quickly try out. Putting into action the suggestions on a consistent basis will lower your blood pressure if this is a problem you face.

OTHER RELATED BOOKS

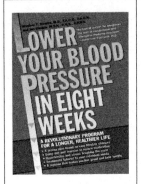

Lower Your Blood Pressure in Eight Weeks

ASIN: B001M5JVQQ
ISBN-13: 978-0345448071

DASH Diet: Slow Cooker Recipes

ASIN: B00TQYTTFI
ISBN-13: 978-1508657743

The Dash Diet Weight Loss Solution

ASIN: B008AS4UR8
ISBN-13: 978-1455512799

Note: The books above are available in both paperback and kindle editions.

Printed in Great Britain
by Amazon

30063363R00050